Developing Literacy
TEXT LEVEL
TEXT-LEVEL ACTIVITIES FOR THE LITERACY HOUR

year

4

Ray Barker

Christine Moorcroft

A & C BLACK

Reprinted 2000
Published 2000 by
A & C Black (Publishers) Limited
35 Bedford Row, London WC1R 4JH

ISBN 0-7136-5319-1

Acknowledgements
The authors and publishers are grateful for permission to reproduce the following:

page 15: extract adapted from *Peter Pan* by permission of Great Ormond Street Hospital for Children;
page 33: extract from 'The End of the Road' by Hilaire Belloc from *Cautionary Verses*,
published by Random House UK Ltd. Reprinted by permission of PFD on behalf of The Estate of Hilaire Belloc
© The Estate of Hilaire Belloc as printed in the original volume;
page 42: extract from 'Milk for the Cat' by Harold Monro by permission of Freda McGregor;
page 60: extract adapted from the leaflet 'Seat Belts and Child Restraints'
issued by the Department of the Environment Transport and the Regions © Crown copyright 1999.

Every effort has been made to trace copyright holders and to obtain their permission for use of copyright material.
The authors and publishers would be pleased to rectify in future editions any error or omission.

The authors and publishers would like to thank the following teachers
for their advice in producing this series of books:

Jane Beynon; Hardip Channa; Ann Hart; Lydia Hunt;
Rita Leader; Madeleine Madden; Helen Mason; Kim Pérez;
Joanne Turpin; Fleur Whatley

A CIP catalogue record for this book is
available from the British Library.

Printed in Great Britain by
St Edmundsbury Press, Ltd, Bury St Edmunds, Suffolk.

Contents

Introduction 4

Fiction and poetry:
reading comprehension
Portrait gallery 9
Character thermometers 10
Details of a setting 11
An imaginary world 12
The passing of time 13
Story mobile 14
Setting out a playscript 15
An author tree 16
Morals in stories 17
An Indian legend 18
A reading review 19
Words to create moods 20
Finding similes 21
A poem from the past 22
Rhyme patterns: 1 23
Rhyme patterns: 2 24
Contrasting poems 25

Fiction and poetry:
writing composition
Haiku chains 26
Cinquain trains 27
Alliteration 28
Couplets 29
Re-writing a poem 30
List poems 31
Conversation poems 32
Powerful verbs 33
Telescope poems 34
Storyboards 35
Plan a character sketch 36

Plan a playscript 37
Six steps for describing 38
Story notes 39
A dilemma 40
Alternative endings 41

Non-fiction:
reading comprehension
Fiction and non-fiction 42
Fact or opinion? 43
A newspaper article 44
Headlines 45
Instructions 46
Arguments 47
Discussions 48
Explanation ladder 49
Advertisements 50
Language to persuade 51
Preparing for research 52
Key words 53
Charts and diagrams 54

Non-fiction:
writing composition
Writing a newspaper article 55
Writing instructions 56
Writing a report 57
Writing an explanation 58
Writing an advertisement 59
Making notes 60
From notes to a paragraph 61
Summarising 62
My point of view 63
A letter to argue 64

Introduction

Developing Literacy: Text Level supports the teaching of reading and writing by providing a series of activities to develop children's ability to recognise and appreciate the different genres, styles and purposes of text. **Year 4** encourages them to read texts from a variety of genres – both non-fiction and fiction, looking at characters, settings and the way narrative is built up. It develops their enjoyment of stories and poetry and provides frameworks which help them to compose their own. It also provides structures on which they can base their non-fiction writing for particular purposes.

The children learn about different kinds of text, including historical and fantasy stories, playscripts, newspaper articles and poems. They are also given the opportunity to encounter everyday texts used in familiar situations (for example, instructions, reports, arguments) as well as to analyse the impact of language in poetry, advertisements and stories from a variety of cultures.

The activities are designed to be carried out in the time allocated to independent work during the Literacy Hour. They support the objectives of the National Literacy Strategy at text level and they incorporate strategies which encourage independent learning – for example, ways in which children can check their own work or that of a partner. Investigation is given greater emphasis as the series progresses towards **Year 6.**

Year 4 helps children to:

- investigate settings and characters in stories and write about them;
- explore chronology and write independently about historical situations;
- explore narrative order and plan stories;
- read and write playscripts;
- look closely at poetic form and write their own poems;
- identify different types of non-fiction text, and comment on content, structure and vocabulary;
- recognise the ways in which texts are written for particular readers;
- describe and review their own reading habits;
- make notes and summarise ideas;
- edit and review their own writing.

Year 4 also develops the children's ability to:

- explore spoken and printed language;
- identify features of non-fiction texts;
- understand and use the terms fact and opinion;
- write in a variety of forms, such as newspaper reports, instructions and non-chronological reports;
- experiment with, and adapt, different forms of poetry;
- understand how descriptive and figurative language can create moods;
- identify and use patterns of rhyme and verse and to write poetry based on particular structures;
- argue a point of view using appropriate language.

Extension

Most of the activity sheets end with a challenge (**Now try this!**) which reinforces and extends the children's learning and provides the teacher with an opportunity for assessment. These more challenging activities might be appropriate for only a few children; it is not expected that the whole class should complete them. On some pages there is space for the children to complete the extension activities, but for others they will need a notebook or separate sheet of paper.

Organisation

Few resources are needed besides scissors, glue, word-banks and a range of dictionaries. The activities have all been designed for use in conjunction with readily available texts of your choice. To help teachers to select appropriate learning experiences for their pupils, the activities are grouped into sections within each book. The pages need not be presented in the order in which they appear in the books, unless otherwise stated.

Teachers' notes

Brief notes are provided at the bottom of most pages. They give ideas and suggestions for making the most of the activity sheet. They sometimes make suggestions for the whole class introduction, the plenary session or, possibly, for follow-up work using an adapted version of the activity sheet.

Structure of the Literacy Hour

The following chart shows an example of the way in which an activity from this book can be used to achieve the required organisation of the Literacy Hour.

Portrait gallery (page 9)

Whole class introduction	15 min
In a shared text which is illustrated, pick out adjectives which describe characters in the pictures. List them, discuss their meanings and ask the children to suggest other words to describe the people. Discuss whether the words tell the reader about the people's character or only about their physical appearance.	

Whole class activity	15 min
Sort the adjectives into categories which suggest favourable and unfavourable views and ask the children for reasons. Use a thesaurus to find other synonyms. Discuss how the synonyms, for example chubby and fat, can suggest a different attitude by the writer.	

Group work	20 min
In pairs, or with the teacher in guided reading time, the children choose characters in their reading book and find adjectives which describe them. They say what the author intends the reader to think about this character, giving reasons.	

Independent work	20 min
The others work independently from **Portrait gallery** (page 9, **Developing Literacy: Text Level Year 4**).	

Whole class plenary session	10 min
The children who have been labelling the portraits should show the pictures and give reasons for the adjectives they have chosen. Encourage discussion of other, more suitable, adjectives. Other groups could give character sketches of the people they have been analysing from reading books. All of this work can lead on to the production of a WANTED poster.	

Using the activity sheets

Fiction and poetry: reading comprehension

Portrait gallery (page 9) introduces the idea that characters are built up from small details, and revises adjectives. It concentrates on factual description whereas **Character thermometers** (page 10) looks at the ways in which feelings about a character can be expressed in descriptions of that character's behaviour or speech. This sheet can be used with any text. The most important feature is that children should always give evidence for their reactions.

Details of a setting (page 11) examines how detail is important when describing settings. Children are asked to identify and categorise various kinds of detail and test their comprehension by saying what is incorrect in a visual representation of the description. This could also serve as a useful model for examining the effect of changing the descriptive details.

An imaginary world (page 12) is particularly useful with science fiction texts or stories about imagined worlds. It gives a framework on which children can structure their thoughts and reactions and develop them into writing compositions. By comparing to film versions of science fiction and fantasy worlds, children should develop their awareness of the issues involved when writers create such worlds. The detail is all-important.

Chronology in narrative can be a very difficult concept for children to grasp. **The passing of time** (page 13) allows the children to map out time passing in a familiar story and notice how special words and phrases can be used to connect the sections. This may help them to move beyond the 'and then... and then...' syndrome when writing narrative!

Story mobile (page 14) provides a format for children to outline and plan their stories. It introduces the concepts of introduction, build-up, climax and resolution.

Setting out a playscript (page 15) is an easy way for children to consider the conventions of a playscript. This sheet could be looked at before a play is studied to introduce the vocabulary or as a way of reinforcing the organisation of a playscript. It is important to show the children that there are reasons for these formalities: the script is meant for performance and the details help the actors and directors to interpret the play.

It is important that the children increase their knowledge of popular authors in order to motivate them to read more. **An author tree** (page 16) helps them to structure their research, perhaps about their favourite author. It leads them to research using other media, for example the Internet, and introduces new vocabulary such as back-cover 'blurb'.

Stories for children of this age are beginning to introduce more 'difficult' issues – dilemmas faced by characters and stories with 'morals'. **Morals in stories** (page 17) uses a fable by AEsop to illustrate the idea of a moral. Children are asked to analyse the structure of the story in order to see more clearly what happens and why. In this way they will be able to identify the lesson of the story. This work could lead on to reading stories from different cultures and finding stories which contain the same kind of moral. **An Indian legend** (page 18) moves them towards this idea. Children should become aware that the ideas and structure of stories from all over the world are similar; it is the small details and cultural beliefs which are different.

It is important to give the children the opportunity to 'sit back' from the books they are reading and be allowed to reflect and review their reading habits. **A reading review** (page 19) gives them the opportunity to be truthful about this. It is important that children give evidence for their views at every stage. This work is developed in **Year 5** and is a useful introduction to reading journals.

The final sheets in this section concern poetry and the use of language to create specific moods and feelings. Most of this work should arise out of shared text work, but these sheets can be used to introduce particular ideas or to provide children with the opportunity to revisit them. **Words to create moods** (page 20) is about the sounds of words, particularly hard- and soft-sounding consonants and vowels. Children should be using specific words to create specific effects, and not just choosing vague words in their writing. **Finding similes** (page 21) shows how comparisons can add vivid detail. The children should be able to identify similes; but more importantly, they should be able to use them for effect in their writing.

A poem from the past (page 22) gives children the opportunity to identify clues to the era in which a poem is written, for example, language use, vocabulary or archaic words.

Rhyme patterns: 1 (page 23) looks closely at couplets, while **Rhyme patterns: 2** (page 24) considers quatrains. Children should be able to identify rhymes and their patterns so that they can write their own verse using these formats.

The original version of Browning's poem, *The Pied Piper of Hamelin*, is:

The Mayor was dumb, and the Council stood
As if they were changed into blocks of wood.

Unable to move a step, or cry
To the children merrily skipping by.

The other couplets are:

There was an old woman, as I have heard tell,
She went to market her eggs for to sell.
(Traditional)

At evening when the lamp is lit,
Around the fire my parents sit. (Longfellow)

And when all were in to the very last,
The door in the mountain-side shut fast.
(Browning)

The original quatrain on page 24 is:

He was a rat, and she was a rat,
And down in one hole they did dwell,
And both were as black as a witch's hat,
And they loved one another well.
(Traditional nursery rhyme)

The other two quatrains are:

Doctor Foster went to Gloucester
In a shower of rain,
He stepped in a puddle, right up to his middle,
And never went there again!
(Traditional nursery rhyme)

She mounted all on her milky white horse
And led her dapple grey,
And rode till she came to her father's house
One hour before it was day. (Traditional ballad)

Finally, **Contrasting poems** (page 25) provides a generic format to help the children compare any poems and note their differences. The children's own views are valid as long as they can support them with evidence from the text.

Fiction and poetry: writing composition

Haiku chains (page 26) and **Cinquain trains** (page 27) help the children to learn about two different patterns in poetry and to use this knowledge to write their own verse. Both of these forms demand a knowledge of syllables – children can clap these and count them out. A haiku has the following syllabic pattern: Line 1: 5 syllables, Line 2: 7 syllables, Line 3: 5 syllables. A cinquain has the following syllabic pattern: Line 1: 2 syllables, Line 2: 4 syllables, Line 3: 6 syllables, Line 4 : 8 syllables, Line 5: 2 syllables.

Alliteration (page 28) helps the children to recognise another pattern through a traditional rhyme; it also gives them a chance to compose using the format and to develop an awareness of the special language terms used in talking about poetry. **Couplets** (page 29) does the same. Both of these sheets revise word-level work.

The original version of the couplets in Christina Rossetti's poem, *What Is Pink?*, is:

> *What is white? A swan is white*
> *Sailing in the light.*
>
> *What is yellow? Pears are yellow,*
> *Rich and ripe and mellow.*
>
> *What is green? The grass is green*
> *With small flowers between.*
>
> *What is violet? Clouds are violet,*
> *In the summer twilight.*
>
> *What is orange? Why, an orange,*
> *Just an orange!*

Re-writing a poem (page 30) can be used when editing and drafting poems. It asks a series of questions which encourage the children to consider their writing; this helps them to re-draft their work.

The following four sheets provide poetry formats for children to consider and upon which to model their writing. They are very simple formats which illustrate the need for pattern and show the children that they can all write successful poems. **List poems** (page 31) follows a simple pattern. **Conversation poems** (page 32) is more sophisticated. The children create a dialogue with another poem. A collection of anthologies is essential for this activity, which the children carry out in pairs. **Powerful verbs** (page 33) uses a well-known poem to illustrate how verbs can be used to create particular effects. This links with sentence-level work. A thesaurus is essential for this activity. **Telescope poems** (page 34) follows a very simple pattern – it draws the reader into a particular focal point and shows the children that poems do not always have to rhyme.

Storyboards (page 35) provides a structure for children to plan their work. It reinforces the vocabulary of introduction, build-up, climax and resolution. The use of pictures helps them to experiment with the structure of their stories. It shows them that it is not always necessary to start with 'Once upon a time' or at the chronological beginning of the narrative. The children can investigate the use of flashback technique and consider what language structures are needed to ensure that the reader understands what is happening, for example phrases such as, '...earlier that day... she never expected...'.

Plan a character sketch (page 36) provides a format for collecting ideas and evidence for writing about any character. This sheet shows that it is not just physical description which makes a character sketch; it is important to reveal what he or she says or does and how these factors influence the way a reader feels about him or her.

Plan a playscript (page 37) helps the children to collect information and ideas for writing playscripts for performance.

The final sheets in this section provide children with various ideas to stimulate writing. **Six steps for describing** (page 38) shows how simple, and often boring statements can be made interesting by adding detail. This sheet also revises sentence-level work on parts of speech. **Story notes** (page 39) shows children how sentences can be edited by deleting the less important parts. **A dilemma** (page 40) gives a series of questions for the children to consider when writing about problems. Such planning formats split situations into the various issues which may arise. It also shows that sometimes there is no 'right answer'. **Alternative endings** (page 41) continues this theme; the children become writers of a well-known story by manipulating its ending.

Non-fiction: reading comprehension

Fiction and non-fiction (page 42) and **Fact or opinion?** (page 43) provide texts for the children to discuss in order to decide how terms should be defined. The terms can be reinforced through reading a variety of texts.

A newspaper article (page 44) and **Headlines** (page 45) continue this work by looking at how newspaper reports follow a particular pattern and layout and the use of headlines in this form. Children can predict newspaper stories from headlines, make notes and then check against the original. Work on newspapers can be easily linked with work in ICT; word processors and desktop publishing can be used. Internet access, for example to the BBC news site, will also give an idea of how news is presented in a variety of media.

Instructions (page 46), **Arguments** (page 47) and **Discussions** (page 48) give children practical opportunities to consider the characteristics of these non-fiction text-types, and **Explanation ladder** (page 49) provides an original format on which to collect ideas and information for explanations. The original order of the instructions on page 46 is:

Ring the nearest fire alarm; Make sure all doors and windows are closed; Leave the building immediately; Ensure no-one is left in the class; Do not stop to collect your bag; Use the nearest safe exit; Walk, do not run; Report to your teacher outside; Line up in the playground; Call the fire brigade.

Work on the media should promote the children's understanding that printed text is not necessarily true, and that language can be manipulated. **Advertisements** (page 50) and **Language to persuade** (page 51) provide activities to illustrate this.

Children are often asked to research a topic and make notes; they need guidance since these processes involve difficult skills. **Preparing for research** (page 52) will help children to formulate their ideas and **Key words** (page 53) and **Charts and** diagrams (page 54) provide simple ways of making notes, and more importantly, putting ideas into their own words. The answers for the activity on page 54 are: Picture 1: Laksmi, Picture 2: Shiva, Picture 3: Brahma, Picture 4: Sarasvati, Picture 5: Vishnu.

Non-fiction: writing composition

Writing a newspaper article (page 55) looks carefully at the features of newspaper articles and provides a format on which the children can plan their ideas.

Writing instructions (page 56) concentrates on the need for writing instructions in chronological order: it is a step-by-step process. A test of good instructions is whether someone can carry them out exactly. In class, this can cause some amusement as children usually miss out important stages! Ask the children to give instructions for drawing an arrangement of two very simple shapes, for example a triangle on top of a circle. See who can draw these correctly following the instructions, and analyse where the instructions go wrong.

Writing a report (page 57) enables the children to plan a report on a particular topic, but the format can be used with any subject area. Focus on the characteristics of reports: the use of present tense, diagrams and organisational devices to help and the use of generalisation. In order to write non-fiction in a way which is clear to the reader, the children need to have a good awareness of the reader's needs. The style and format of their writing should take these needs into account. **Writing an explanation** (page 58) shows this. The children have to explain a complex process from a picture.

Writing an advertisement (page 59) examines the features of advertisements and provides a format on which children can plan their ideas. This can also be used as a checklist for research. The children could watch advertisements to notice which features they contain and how they use language to persuade.

The next three sheets provide opportunities for the children to make and use notes in a variety of ways. **Making notes** (page 60) asks them to put notes from sentences into a chart. **From notes to a paragraph** (page 61) takes abbreviated notes and asks the children to put them into another form. **Summarising** (page 62) shows how notes can be made by underlining and extracting only the essential points.

Finally, two writing formats are provided to help the children to express their own views. **My point of view** (page 63) asks for evidence to back up a point of view. **A letter to argue** (page 64) both introduces the letter format and shows how an effective argument can be structured.

Glossary of terms used

alliteration The repetition of a letter or phoneme at the beginning of words in a phrase, for example: *Peter Piper picked a peck of pickled peppers.*
chronology A sequence of events in time, from Chronos, the God of Time.
cinquain A poem of five lines with a specific syllabic pattern: 2, 4, 6, 8, 2. Invented by Adelaide Crapsey in the 1920s.
couplet Two consecutive lines of poetry which rhyme.
discussion text A text which gives all sides of an issue. It can be written or spoken.
explanatory text A text which explains a process or answers a question.
figurative language Language which is not literal (factual), for example, simile and metaphor. Such language is used to create mood or atmosphere.
genre A specific type of writing or other medium of communication, for example: legend, newspaper story or poem.
haiku A poem of three lines with a specific syllabic pattern: 5, 7, 5. This is an ancient Japanese poetic form.
instructional text A text which gives the reader information to be able to carry out some aim, for example, to make something or to reach a particular place. Instructions use the imperative (command) form of the verb.
narrative A text which retells events or a story, often in chronological order.
onomatopoeia The use of words which echo sounds associated with their meaning, for example: *bang, boom, squeak.*
playscript A text written to be performed. The format of a playscript is designed to make actors and directors interpret the text for performance, hence the inclusions of stage directions and clues for more effective performance.
quatrain A four-lined poem or verse of a poem which rhymes in a particular sequence.
recount A text (or part of a text) usually written in the past tense, to re-tell for information or entertainment. It uses descriptive language and might include dialogue.
report A non-chronological text, usually written in the present tense, that describes or classifies.
rhyme When words contain the same sound in their last syllables, for example: *go/slow, say/grey.*
scan To look at a text quickly, locating key words and ideas.
simile A comparison of two things using 'like' or 'as'. This aims to create a picture in the reader's mind.
skim To read a passage to gain an initial overview of the subject matter.

Portrait gallery

- **Describe each character using words from the word-bank.**

Check the meanings of any words which are new to you.

_____
_____
_____
_____
_____

_____
_____
_____
_____

_____
_____
_____
_____

_____
_____
_____
_____

Word-bank

Eyebrows:
arched
bushy
straight

Eyes:
hooded eyelids
small
round

Noses:
bumpy
hooked
long
snub

Mouths:
downturned
thin and small
wide

Chins:
pointed
round with a cleft
square

Faces:
freckled
round
square
thin
wide

- **Draw a picture of a character for a 'WANTED' poster. Use the words on this sheet to write a description.**

Teachers' note You could ask the class to imagine that one of their friends is missing and they need to write a police description. Discuss what features need to be described and how they would describe the person accurately. Distinguish between the physical description of character and how a character acts and behaves. Discuss what conclusions people draw from physical description.

Developing Literacy
Text Level Year 4
© A & C Black 2000

Character thermometers

- **Record your thoughts about characters in a text.**

Example:

Character: The Wolf in 'Little Red Riding Hood'

kind		cruel

Evidence from the text
The wolf is very cruel as he eats Grandma and wants to kill Little Red Riding Hood.

Add your own words to the word-bank.

Character:

Evidence from the text

Character:

Evidence from the text

Character:

Evidence from the text

Word-bank
brave
cruel
foolish
kind
selfish

- **Use your evidence to write how you feel about each character.**

Now try this!

Teachers' note You could extend this activity by producing large character thermometers to display in class. Use the opportunity to collect the characteristics gathered by the children and allow them to sort them into opposites, for example, kind–cruel. Discuss how the same evidence or behaviour can be seen in a different light by different people.

Developing Literacy
Text Level Year 4
© A & C Black 2000

Details of a setting

• **Read the description. Write three details in each notepad.**

It was warm for April. I could hear the church bells calling people to midday prayers. High above the mountain fir trees I could see the large stone castle. It was square and made from huge blocks of stone. It had four pointed turrets, one at each corner. Around the top of the castle walls the stones were laid to look like jagged teeth. Ten soldiers, wearing shiny armour, were walking on the walls. Their horses were feeding on grass outside. The wooden drawbridge, in the middle of the wall facing the road, was down. There was a wide moat, full of water. Three ducks were swimming on the smooth water. We were ready to attack.

Details about the castle	Details about the time, season and weather	Details about people
made of stone		

• **List six things which are wrong in this picture of the setting.**

Now try this!

• **Change the detail in the text. Write a description of the same castle, at night in winter.**

Teachers' note Model with the children how to extract relevant details. Discuss what the description of the setting would be like without the use of accurate details. How much are they told (for example, about the season, and the time of day), without actually stating the facts? Experiment with changing details to become aware of how consistency of detail is important in writing.

Developing Literacy
Text Level Year 4
© A & C Black 2000

An imaginary world

- **Look at this picture of an imaginary world.**
- **Answer the questions.**

What would I see?

What would I hear?

What would I feel?

What would I smell?

What sort of people might live there?

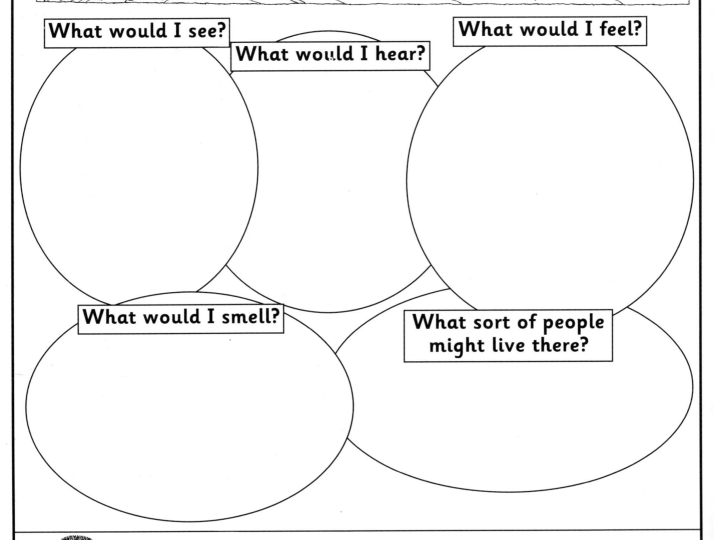

- **Write five paragraphs about the imaginary world.**
  Use your notes.

Teachers' note This technique can be used for any setting, but here it is particularly useful for the science fiction genre. Children could devise a survey to analyse the settings of TV science fiction series and could write stories or scripts containing the elements they have identified. The aim is for children to understand the importance of consistent use of relevant detail in their writing.

Developing Literacy
Text Level Year 4
© A & C Black 2000

The passing of time

These pictures tell the story of *Sleeping Beauty*.

- Cut out the pictures. Put them in the right order.
- Cut out the captions and match them to the pictures.

Then one day a prince...	When she was born...	They lived happily ever after...
Once upon a time...	When she was eighteen...	One hundred years passed...
Her childhood passed by...	He fought his way...	They had forgotten to invite...

- **Write the whole story in the correct order. Use phrases which show how time has passed.**

Teachers' note Discuss the original story with the children. Model how each of the sections of the story would be introduced by specific words or phrases which would show time passing, for example, then... after a hundred years, and so on. Experiment with telling the story in a different order. Does this still show how time passes? Discuss the effect of this on telling the story.

Developing Literacy
Text Level Year 4
© A & C Black 2000

Story mobile

• **Use the mobile to plan a story of your own.**

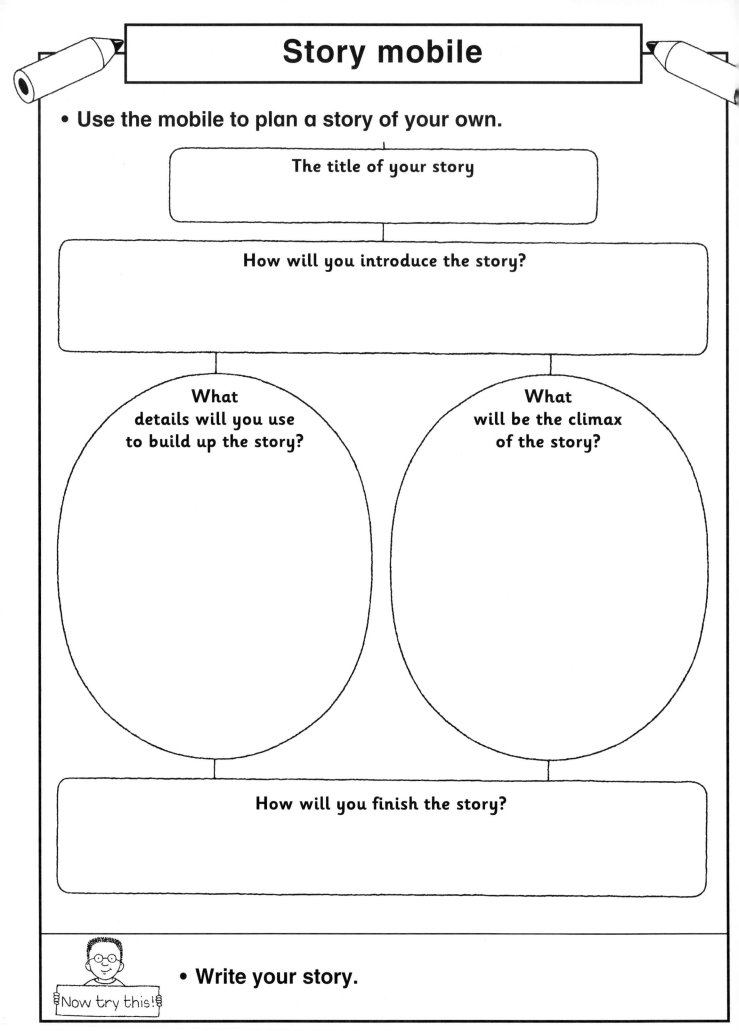

The title of your story

How will you introduce the story?

What details will you use to build up the story?

What will be the climax of the story?

How will you finish the story?

• **Write your story.**

Now try this!

Teachers' note Children could make mobiles to hang in the class. In this way they could compare the different kinds of detail which make story structure interesting. Ask them to analyse how many different kinds of stories they can find and then write a variety of stories using similar structures. This leads on to work on genre.

Developing Literacy
Text Level Year 4
© A & C Black 2000

Setting out a playscript

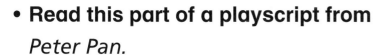

- **Read this part of a playscript from** *Peter Pan.*
- **Write labels in the boxes to show how the play is set out. Use the checklist to help you.**

ACT I Scene i

The bedroom of the three Darling children: John, Michael and Wendy. The year is 1890. There are three beds and a basket for Nana, the dog, in the room.

Enter Peter Pan, flying.

PETER: *(Whispering)* Tinker Bell, where are you? *(A light shines from an open drawer in a chest.)*
TINK: *(A tinkle of bells ...)* I'm over here.
PETER: Have you found my lost shadow?
TINK: Yes, it's in the box over there.
(Peter moves to it.)
PETER: Ah! Here it is. *(He picks up his shadow, rolled up neatly. He tries to stick it back on. He cannot. He sits on the floor and cries.)*

Wendy wakes up. She sits up and sees Peter.

WENDY: Why are you crying, little boy?
(Peter jumps up and bows.)
PETER: Was it you who found my shadow? What is your name?

- **Make a list of the props and costumes that you would need to perform this part of the script.**

Now try this!

Props	Costumes

- **Do the same for another playscript.**

Teachers' note Model with the children what makes a playscript different from other texts in its layout. Discuss the reasons for these features. It is important for children to realise that a play is written primarily for performance and not for reading from the page. Performing the script and taking on different roles, such as director and costume designer, will help them to appreciate this.

Developing Literacy
Text Level Year 4
© A & C Black 2000

An author tree

Author: _____

Nationality: _____

Alive or dead: _____

Books written (with dates):

To find information I used:

CD-ROMs ☐

The Internet ☐

Reference books ☐

Back-cover 'blurbs' ☐

Other ☐

_____

_____

_____

_____

_____

Best-known books:

Subjects of books:

Personal details:

Where he/she lives or lived

What the author did before he/she became a writer

Now try this!

- **Collect information on** authors from one country or authors of one kind of book.
- **Discuss your findings with a partner.**

Teachers' note Children could collect together their 'trees' and publish them as books. They could devise categories for the selection, for example, authors from America, or authors who write about space travel. Large author trees could be made for display in class. Children could find photographs of their favourite authors and explain why they like their books so much.

**Developing Literacy
Text Level Year 4
© A & C Black 2000**

Morals in stories

- **Read this fable by Aesop.**

The Lion and the Mouse

A mighty lion was sleeping in the jungle. A tiny mouse, not looking where she was going, ran over the lion's nose and woke him up. The lion clapped his enormous paw on the tiny mouse.

The mouse squealed and begged for mercy. 'Forgive me, King of the Jungle, I was so busy looking for food that I did not notice your nose. I must get home to my children or they will starve.' She quivered and cried. The lion saw that she meant no harm. He took pity on her and let her go.

Now, not long after, the lion fell into a trap laid by hunters. He let out a roar which filled the whole jungle. The mouse heard it. She ran to the trap. Straight away she nibbled at the rope in the trap and soon the lion was free.

- **Draw what happens in the story in the boxes.**

At the start the mouse...	Then the lion...	The lion later...	And the mouse...

- **What lesson does this story teach you? This is called the** `moral`.

_____

_____

- **Write a story about today's world to teach the same moral.**

Now try this!

Teachers' note Read the story with the children to distinguish the four stages in the narrative. Notice what the characters are like in each section and ask the children how their characters are changing and why. Extract the moral by questioning. You could discuss the morals of other fables.

Developing Literacy
Text Level Year 4
© A & C Black 2000

An Indian legend

This legend from India has been muddled up!

- **Cut out the sections. Put them in the right order.**

Why Ganesh has an elephant's head

The goddess Parvati was married to the god Shiva. They lived in the Himalaya mountains. Parvati was lonely. She wanted someone to talk to. Her husband was away for years. He was either creating and destroying, or dancing on the top of the world to keep it moving around.

Seeing Parvati's distress, Shiva promised to go into the forest and cut off the head of the first living thing he saw. Then he would bring it back. Next he would fit it onto the head of the child and bring it back to life. That is what he did, but... the first thing he saw was an elephant. That is why Ganesh, the god of wisdom, has an elephant's head. He only has one tusk... but that is another story.

As Parvati was bathing, Shiva returned. He heard his wife splashing in the river. He walked towards her, but the little boy stopped him.
'Don't go any further,' he shouted.
Now Shiva did not know about the child. And he was not used to being told what to do. So he took out his sword and chopped off the boy's head.

She loved that child. He grew up and they were never separated. One day, Parvati wanted to take a bath in the river. She told her son to keep guard.
'Don't worry, mother, I shall let no-one near you,' he promised.

Parvati heard the noise and came running.
'You have murdered my child!' she screamed.

One day, she was playing in the muddy river. She had an idea.
'I can make a child out of clay and use magic to make it live,' she said. So she made a little, fat mud-baby and put it out to dry. The sun woke it up.

Now try this!

- **What tells you that this story is from India?**

Copy and complete the chart.

Names	Places	What people believe

Teachers' note In the plenary session you could discuss what happens in the legend and identify those features which obviously make it a story from India. Children could find other stories from India; this could link with RE.

Developing Literacy
Text Level Year 4
© A & C Black 2000

A reading review

Name _____

Class _____

Date _____

Cross out the words you don't need.

I think reading is important because...

_____
_____
_____
_____
_____

I enjoy/do not enjoy reading because...

_____
_____
_____
_____
_____

The last three books I read were...

_____
_____
_____
_____
_____

I prefer fiction/non-fiction because...

_____
_____
_____
_____
_____

My favourite author is...

_____

My favourite book is... I like it because...

_____
_____
_____
_____

Now try this!

- Use your notes to write a longer piece about how you feel about reading.

Teachers' note Discuss the reasons for writing a reading review and why the various sections of the review are important, for example, why is it important to add the date? Children should be made aware of the features of the review and the kind and quality of information and personal response required.

Developing Literacy
Text Level Year 4
© A & C Black 2000

Words to create moods

Some words can give you a sense of what an object or a place is like. They create a mood .

- **Choose words which give you the idea of a piece of broken glass. Write them in the shape.**

Short, sharp, hard-sounding words create this mood.

- **Write words which give you the idea of a cloud.**

Long, smooth, soft-sounding words create this mood.

Now try this!

- **Write three more words to suit the mood of each shape.**
- **Use five of the words from the word-bank in sentences.**

Teachers' note This could link with word-level work on, for example, hard and soft consonants. Children should exaggerate the sounds of the words to experience the hard and the soft sounds which create the different moods. You could extend this activity to build up class word-banks to categorise the kinds of words children think of to create different moods.

Developing Literacy
Text Level Year 4
© A & C Black 2000

Finding similes

When you describe something using the words 'like' or 'as', you are writing a simile. You are comparing one thing to something else.

- Read the poem.

The Bear

He needs:
A coat like thick brown moss,
A head like a sculptured rock,
Claws like metal combs,
Paws like boxing gloves,
And a growl like rumbling thunder.

ANONYMOUS

- **Underline five things a bear needs.**
- **Circle what these are compared to.**
- **Which word is left in each line?**
- **Complete the chart.**

What a bear needs	It is compared to...	The simile makes me think of...
a coat	thick brown moss	something soft – moss is soft

Now try this!

- **Write similes about:** the snow , stars in the sky , noisy traffic , a plate of chips **and** the teeth of a shark .

Use 'like' or 'as'.

Teachers' note The children could collect similes on one particular subject and write simile poems like the one above. The most important aspect of this work is not just that the children can identify similes but also that they can see how using them can enrich description.

Developing Literacy
Text Level Year 4
© A & C Black 2000

A poem from the past

This is part of a long poem. It was written in the 1850s.

• Read the poem.

> Once more he stept into the street;
>   And to his lips again
> Laid his long pipe of smooth straight cane;
>   And ere he blew three notes (such sweet
> Soft notes as yet musician's cunning
>   Never gave the enraptured air)
> There was a rustling that seem'd like a bustling
> Of merry crowds justling at pitching and hustling,
> Small feet were pattering, wooden shoes clattering,
> Little hands clapping, and little tongues chattering,
> And, like fowls in a farm-yard when barley is
>   scattering,
> Out came the children running.
> All the little boys and girls,
> With rosy cheeks and flaxen curls,
> And sparkling eyes and teeth like pearls,
> Tripping and skipping, ran merrily after
> The wonderful music with shouting and laughter.

FROM *The Pied Piper of Hamelin* BY ROBERT BROWNING

• How can you tell it was written more than 100 years ago?

• Copy and complete the chart.

Words which sound old-fashioned	Words I have never seen before	Strange expressions – the way words are put together
ere	stept	merry crowds justling at pitching and hustling

• Find the meaning of some of these words and expressions. Write a modern version of the story.

Use a dictionary.

Teachers' note Ensure that the children know the story of the Pied Piper before they tackle this activity. This work links with word-level objectives – word derivation, how language has changed and the use of a variety of dictionaries. The children should become aware that the language itself should not become a barrier to their enjoyment of a text.

Developing Literacy
Text Level Year 4
© A & C Black 2000

Rhyme patterns: 1

Two lines of poetry which rhyme are
called a ⬚couplet⬚.

Think of the word 'couple', meaning two.

* **Read these couplets.**
* **Underline the words which rhyme.**

There was an old woman who lived in a shoe;
She had so many children, she didn't know what to do.

No stir in the air, no stir in the sea,
The ship was as still as she could be.

Notice where in the lines the rhymes come.

They fought for hours of the day.
At length that wild hog stole away.

* **Add rhymes to complete these couplets from**
The Pied Piper of Hamelin.

The Mayor was dumb, and the Council stood
As if they were changed into blocks of _____

Unable to move a step, or cry
To the children merrily skipping_____

* **Write out these lines to make three couplets.**

There was an old woman, as I have had heard tell,

The door in the mountain-side shut fast.

At evening when the lamp is lit,

She went to market her eggs for to sell.

Around the fire my parents sit.

And when all were in to the very last,

Now try this!

* **Write your own couplet. Use a first line from this sheet.**

Teachers' note To introduce the activity you could model the first example, asking the children where the rhymes come in the lines and how many lines there are. Rhymes are useful in word-level work as they often use the same sound for words which are spelled differently, for example, sea/be; shoe/do. Children could look for couplets in anthologies, (an opportunity to read more poetry).

Developing Literacy
Text Level Year 4
© A & C Black 2000

Rhyme patterns: 2

A |quatrain| is a verse that has four lines which rhyme.

- **Read these quatrains.**
- **Underline the words which rhyme.**

Think of the word 'quarter', meaning four.

> Mary, Mary, quite contrary,
> How does your garden grow?
> With silver bells and cockle shells,
> And pretty maids all in a row.

> I hear in the chamber above me
> The patter of little feet,
> The sound of a door that is opened,
> And voices soft and sweet.

Notice where in the lines the rhymes come.

- **Write some rhymes to complete this quatrain:**

> He was a rat, and she was a rat,
> And down in one hole they did dwell,
> And both were as black as a witch's _____
> And they loved one another _____

- **Write out these lines to make two quatrains.**

Doctor Foster went to Gloucester

And never went there again!

And rode till she came to her father's house

She mounted all on her milky white horse

In a shower of rain,

One hour before it was day.

And led her dapple grey,

He stepped in a puddle, right up to his middle,

Now try this!

- **Write your own quatrain. Use a first line from this sheet.**

Teachers' note To introduce this activity you could model the first example, asking the children where the rhymes come in the lines and how many lines there are. Rhymes are useful in word-level work as they often use the same sound for words which are spelled differently, for example, boat/note. Children could look for quatrains in anthologies, (an opportunity to read more poetry).

Developing Literacy
Text Level Year 4
© A & C Black 2000

Contrasting poems

- Use this chart to help you write about the differences between two poems.

	Titles	When written
1.		
2.		

- Complete the chart.

	Poem 1	Poem 2
What is the poem about?		
Does the poem rhyme?		
Is there a rhyme pattern? Give examples.		
Is each poem serious or funny?		
Is the language simple or difficult? Give examples.		

Which poem do you like best? _____

Why?_____

_____

Now try this!

- Use your notes to write about the two poems. Explain how they are different. What do you like or dislike about them?

Teachers' note The children may find that obvious comparisons are the best to discuss in the first instance, for example, they could use a limerick about an animal to contrast with a more serious approach. Stress that children's own views about poetry are valid as long as they can give evidence from the text.

Developing Literacy
Text Level Year 4
© A & C Black 2000

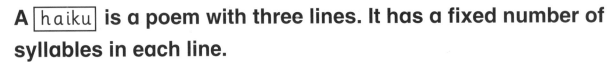

Haiku chains

A ⌈haiku⌉ is a poem with three lines. It has a fixed number of syllables in each line.

- **Read this haiku.**
- **Write each syllable of the haiku in a link of the chain.**
- **Write the number of syllables in each line in the box.**

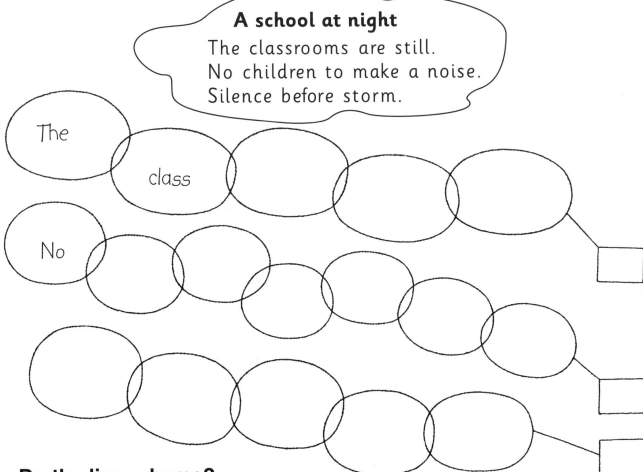

A school at night
The classrooms are still.
No children to make a noise.
Silence before storm.

The · class · No

- **Do the lines rhyme?** _____
- **Complete this haiku.**

A school in the morning
First in the playground

_____

_____

The first line
has been
written for you.

Now try this!

- **Write another haiku about a game you play in the playground.**

Teachers' note Model with the children how to count the syllables. Bring out the simple introduction followed by a poet's statement and a final surprise in the last line. Stress the importance of the poetic form; this poem is not rhymed but is rigid in its form. You could collect the children's poems to make into a haiku book called *Children's Games.*

Developing Literacy
Text Level Year 4
© A & C Black 2000

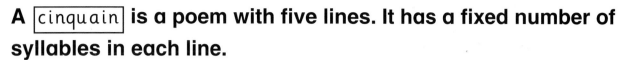

Cinquain trains

A ⟨cinquain⟩ is a poem with five lines. It has a fixed number of syllables in each line.

- **Read this cinquain.**
- **Write each syllable of the cinquain in a train carriage.**
- **In the box, write the number of syllables in each line.**

> Christmas.
> Lights on the tree.
> Children hoping for snow.
> All the presents tied in bright bows.
> Waiting.

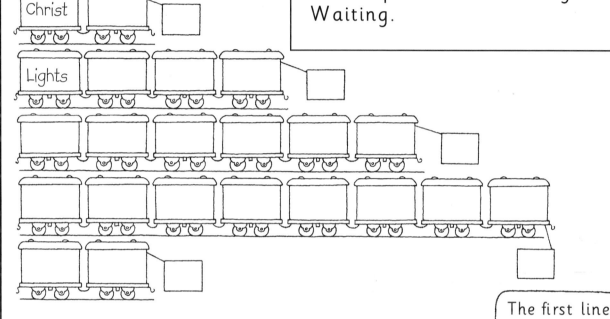

- **Do the lines rhyme?** _____
- **Complete this cinquain:**

  Monday. _____

  _____

  _____

  _____

  _____

> The first line has been written for you.

- **Write a cinquain about another day of the week.**

Teachers' note Model with the children how to count the syllables. Bring out the idea that the poems are like a piece of elastic: they stretch and become narrower again. Stress the importance of the poetic form; this poem is not rhymed but is rigid in its form. You could collect the children's cinquains to make a books called *Cinquain Calendar*.

Developing Literacy
Text Level Year 4
© A & C Black 2000

Alliteration

Tongue-twisters use alliteration**. This is when words begin with the same letter over and over again.**

- **Try saying this tongue-twister. Underline the letter which is repeated.**

Peter Piper picked a peck of pickled peppers;
A peck of pickled peppers Peter Piper picked;
If Peter Piper picked a peck of pickled peppers,
Where's the peck of pickled peppers Peter
                                    Piper picked?

- **Complete this alliteration poem about animals.**

One   wet   walrus   waggled   his   whiskers.

Two   tigers

Three   thrushes

Four   ferrets

Five

Six

Seven

Eight

Nine

Ten

- **Write another poem which has a number at the start of each line. In each line, make as many words as possible begin with the same letter.**

Teachers' note Have fun with the tongue-twister and ask the children for more examples. These could be collected into a shared text. It is important to link this with word-level work in that the children should realise that making the same sound does not always involve using the same letters.

Developing Literacy
Text Level Year 4
© A & C Black 2000

Couplets

- **Read the poem. It is written in couplets.**

What is pink? A rose is pink
By the fountain's brink.

What is red? A poppy's red
In its barley bed.

What is blue? The sky is blue
Where the clouds float through.

FROM *What is pink?* BY CHRISTINA ROSSETTI

- **Match the lines of these couplets and write them out correctly.**

What is yellow? Pears are yellow	Sailing in the light.
What is violet? Clouds are violet	With small flowers between.
What is green? The grass is green	Rich and ripe and mellow.
What is white? A swan is white	In the summer twilight.

_____   _____

_____   _____

_____   _____

- **Write two more couplets about the colours black and grey.**

Think of things which are these colours.

Now try this!

- **The last couplet of the poem begins,** *What is orange?* **Complete the couplet using your own words.**

Teachers' note Remind the children about the characteristics of this poetic form (see page 23). Identify the rhyming words in each couplet. Discuss how some rhyming words make the same sound but are spelled differently, for example, white/light. Use the discussion of couplets to introduce the concept of rhythm in a line of poetry, and count out the beats in each line.

Developing Literacy
Text Level Year 4
© A & C Black 2000

Re-writing a poem

- **Use this chart to improve a poem you have written.**

This page helps you to make sure your poem says what you want it to say.

Title _____

I am not happy with these lines	I shall change them to...

Interesting comparisons in my poem	Other comparisons I could make

Rhymes which I could improve	Changed rhymes

Use a rhyming dictionary.

- **Re-draft your poem.**
- **Ask a partner to read it aloud. Are you happy with it?**
- **Make any other changes which would improve your poem.**

Now try this!

Teachers' note The object of drafting a poem is to find out what the child wants to write and for him/her to write it better. One of the best ways to do this is to ask questions to help clarify what is trying to be achieved and what, in language terms, can be written to achieve it.

Developing Literacy
Text Level Year 4
© A & C Black 2000

List poems

- **Read the poem. Can you work out the pattern?**

1. This is the house that Jack built.

2. This is the malt
   That lay in the house that Jack built.

3. This is the rat
   That ate the malt
   That lay in the house that Jack built.

4. This is the cat
   That kill'd the rat
   That ate the malt
   That lay in the house that Jack built.

- **Here is the start of the fifth verse. Write the next three lines. Draw the picture in the box.**

5. This is the dog
   That worried the cat,

   _____

   _____

   _____

- **Continue the poem on a separate sheet of paper, following the pattern.**

  Here are the beginnings of the next three verses:

    This is the cow…
    This is the maiden…
    This is the man…

Now try this!

- **Write a list poem using the days of the week or the months of the year.**

On Monday…
On Tuesday…

Teachers' note Making lists is a simple way for children to assemble words and ideas and build their vocabulary. Try collecting captions, for example, about animals, and displaying them as a collage. Numbers are useful for list poems. Children could write time poems, for example, at one o'clock… at two o'clock… or could use the song 'Ten Green Bottles' as a model.

Developing Literacy
Text Level Year 4
© A & C Black 2000

Conversation poems

- **Read this conversation poem.**

The summer leaves twitch and whisper
I've never heard them talking
They talk in the branches
What? Just amongst themselves?
Some whistle or sing
They must be happy in the summer
They call for light
They need the light
To the sun
It's bright overhead
Or to the clouds
Look out! The rain's coming!
They need refreshing rain
It feeds their tree
Rain wets the face of the leaves
The leaves drip with happiness.

- **Underline in** red **all the words of one speaker.**

- **Underline in** blue **all the words of the other speaker.**

- **What do you notice about the pattern of a conversation poem?**

_____

- **Write a conversation with this poem.**

As I walked in the streets of Laredo,

_____

As I walked out in the streets one day,

_____

I spied a young cowboy all wrapped in white linen,

_____

All wrapped in white linen as cold as the clay.

_____

- **Continue the conversation.**

Teachers' note This kind of activity promotes paired writing. This ensures a greater level of contribution from each individual but gives a smaller, more supportive audience for the less confident. Try writing question and answer poems. One child sets a question and his/her partner must respond with an imaginative answer. They then take it in turns.

Developing Literacy
Text Level Year 4
© A & C Black 2000

Powerful verbs

- **Read this poem, which describes a long walk.**

The End of the Road

In these boots and with this staff
Two hundred leaguers and a half
Walked I, went I, paced I, tripped I,
Marched I, held I, skelped* I, slipped I,   * slapped
Pushed I, panted, swung and dashed I;
Picked I, forded, swam and splashed I,
Strolled I, climbed I, crawled and scrambled,
Dropped and dipped I, ranged and rambled;
Plodded I, hobbled I, trudged and tramped I...

HILAIRE BELLOC

- **Underline the verbs in the poem.**
- **In the boot, write the verbs which say the same as 'walking'.**

-  **Continue this poem, following the same pattern as Hilaire Belloc. Imagine you are running for a bus, or running to school because you are late.**

In these boots and in this sun
A hundred metres I have run,
Chased I, puffed I, galloped I, tripped I...

Use a thesaurus.

Teachers' note Revise verbs as action words. Children could list as many verbs as possible to describe walking across the classroom. After reading the poem, compare the two lists. Discuss how more accurate verbs give a better impression in a description. Discuss alternatives for 'got' and 'went'.

Developing Literacy
Text Level Year 4
© A & C Black 2000

Telescope poems

- **Read this extract from a poem. Can you work out the pattern?**

This is the key of the kingdom:
In that kingdom there is a city;
In that city is a town;
In that town there is a street;
In that street there winds a lane;
In that lane there is a yard;
In that yard there is a house;
In that house there waits a room;
In that room an empty bed;
And on that bed a basket –
A basket of sweet flowers.

TRADITIONAL

- **Underline the objects. Which is biggest? Which is smallest?**

- **In the diagram, write the things in the poem in order of size. Begin with the largest. Make your writing smaller and smaller!**

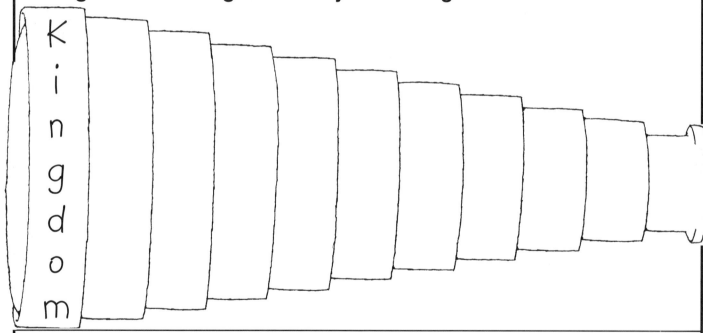

K
i
n
g
d
o
m

Now try this!

- **Imagine you are standing on a hill and looking through a telescope at a city. Write a poem, describing what you see. Start with the whole city, and get smaller and smaller until you are looking through a window into a room.**

Teachers' note Model the structure with the children, making them aware that the objects mentioned become smaller and smaller. You could use the opposite view as well – as if looking through a microscope.

Developing Literacy
Text Level Year 4
© A & C Black 2000

Storyboards

- **Look carefully at the picture story.**
- **What happens in the end? Draw the final box.**

- **Use the storyboards to plan the story in note form.**

Writing captions for the pictures will help.

Introduction	The build-up

The climax	The end

- **Write the story from the information in your storyboards.**

Teachers' note Model the various stages in writing a story. Encourage the children to use captions as well as spending their time drawing, as they will be able to remember their story ideas more easily. Discuss what the effect of changing the structure of their story world be, for example, if they started at the exciting climax. How would they make links with the rest of the structure?

Developing Literacy
Text Level Year 4
© A & C Black 2000

Plan a character sketch

- **Use this page to help you write a character sketch.**

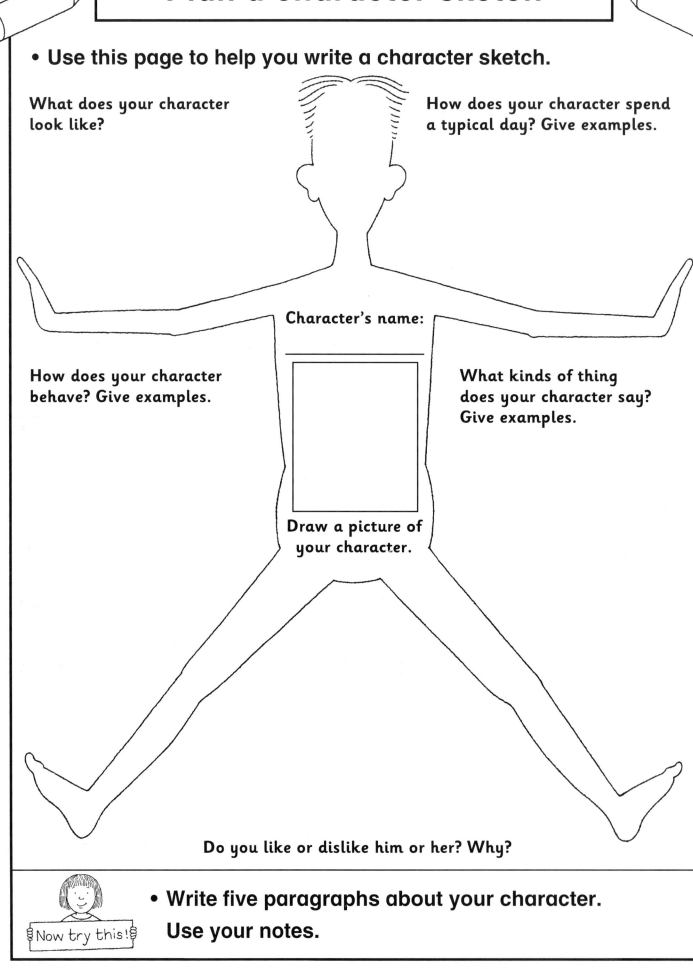

What does your character look like?

How does your character spend a typical day? Give examples.

Character's name:

_____

How does your character behave? Give examples.

What kinds of thing does your character say? Give examples.

Draw a picture of your character.

Do you like or dislike him or her? Why?

- **Write five paragraphs about your character. Use your notes.**

Now try this!

Teachers' note This sheet could be used to structure a response to a character in a text the children have been reading, or to form the basis of a character study which could then be included in a piece of creative writing. A group could write about the characters in one particular text and collect the sheets into a book.

Developing Literacy
Text Level Year 4
© A & C Black 2000

Plan a playscript

• **Plan a well-known nursery rhyme or fable as a playscript.**

Title _____

Characters in my play	The setting of my play

The story of my play	How many acts or scenes will be needed

What costumes will be needed	What scenery will be needed

Now try this!

• **Write the playscript.**

Teachers' note The children should complete page 15 before they tackle this activity. Use a playscript you are reading as a shared text to itemise all the features of a playscript. Bring the children to an awareness that the script is written to be performed and the features indicate this. When children perform their plays, ask the rest of the class to discuss the performance critically.

Developing Literacy
Text Level Year 4
© A & C Black 2000

Six steps for describing

'The man walked down the road' is a very boring sentence.
These six steps can make it more interesting.

1. | **Use an adjective:** | The (tall) man walked down the road.

2. | **Use another adjective:** | The tall, (thin) man walked down the road.

3. | **Change the verb into a more exciting one:** | The tall, thin man (limped) down the road.

4. | **Use an adverb:** | The tall, thin man limped (slowly) down the road.

5. | **Give an ending:** | The tall, thin man limped slowly down the road on (his journey home.)

6. | **Use an adjective in the ending:** | The tall, thin man limped slowly down the road on his (long) journey home.

Use the six steps.

• **Write your own description.**

Starting sentence _____

1. _____
2. _____
3. _____

4. _____

5. _____

6. _____

Now try this!

• **Add a** | simile | **to your description.**

_____

_____

Teachers' note This is an opportunity to revise word-level work on parts of speech and to put into context why it is important to have an awareness of them. Discuss what extra information is given in the description and how this affects the picture given to the reader. Encourage the children to edit their descriptions, writing them in shorter sentences.

Developing Literacy
Text Level Year 4
© A & C Black 2000

Story notes

• **Read the notes for the story of** *The Princess and the Pea*.

Once upon a time – prince – wanted to marry princess – travelled all over – could not find real ps. – none quite right – home. Storm – knocking on gate – a ps. – soaked – said she wanted to marry p. – Queen made test – 3 peas under 20 mattresses – 10 feather beds on top – ps. to sleep in bed – would she feel the peas? – real ps. would – morning – ps. had bad night – felt peas – showed bruises – only true ps. so tender – p. married her – lived happily ever after.

• **Write three things which show these are notes.**

1. <u>The writer does not use complete sentences.</u>

2. _____

3. _____

• **Write the story of** *The Princess and the Pea* **using proper sentences.**

_____

_____

_____

_____

_____

_____

Turn over to finish your story.

• **Read another fairy tale or folk tale. Make notes from it for a partner. Ask your partner to write the story in full.**

Teachers' note This work links closely with word-level objectives on shortening words and on sentence-level objectives concerning shortening sentences without altering meaning. List various abbreviations and ways of making notes, such as the use of dashes. The children should be shown how to focus on the important aspects of the storyline, not on the extraneous detail.

Developing Literacy
Text Level Year 4
© A & C Black 2000

A dilemma

- **Look carefully at the picture.**
- **Imagine you had to face this dilemma.**

A dilemma is a problem. You have to decide what to do.

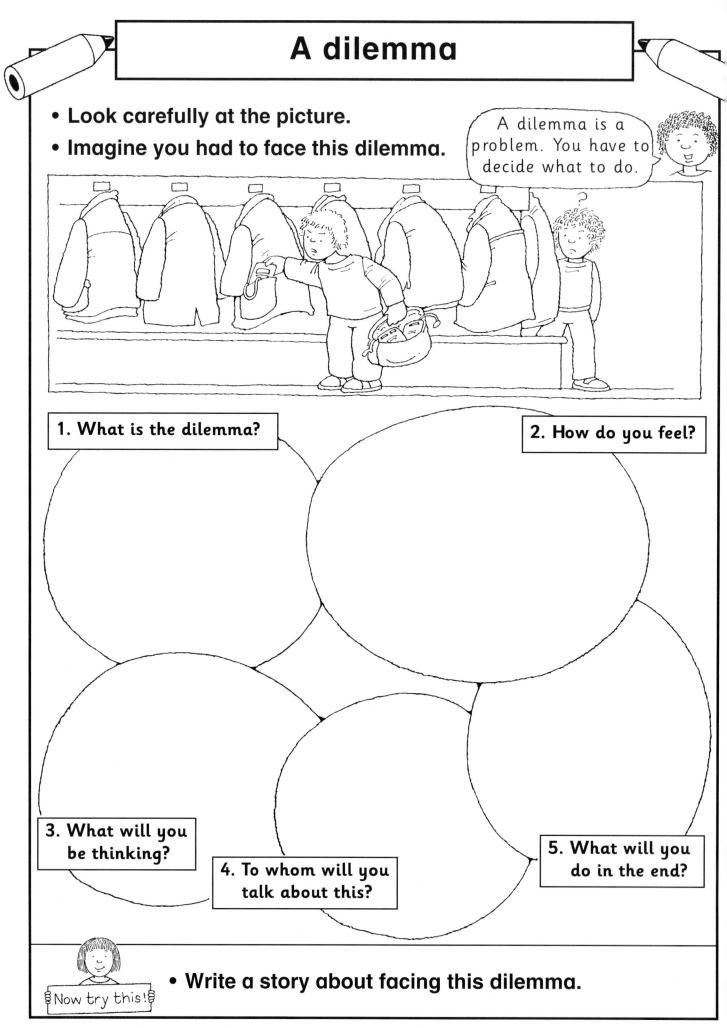

1. What is the dilemma?

2. How do you feel?

3. What will you be thinking?

4. To whom will you talk about this?

5. What will you do in the end?

Now try this!

- **Write a story about facing this dilemma.**

Teachers' note As with most real-life school settings, sometimes dilemmas have to be treated with sensitivity. However this sheet and its approach can be adapted to any dilemma. Find dilemmas in shared texts. Stop when reading them and ask the children what they think characters will do next and why. They should be able to back up their answers with evidence from the text.

Developing Literacy
Text Level Year 4
© A & C Black 2000

Alternative endings

- **Look carefully at the story of** *Little Red Riding Hood*.
- **Decide what is happening in each storyboard.**

| Introduction to the story | The build-up of the story | The climax of the story | The end of the story – the resolution |

- **Choose an ending from one of these pictures.**

Think about how each ending would change the story.

- **When you have chosen your ending, and thought about what will happen, write your story.**

Now try this!

- **Use one of the other endings and write the story. How does the different ending change the rest of the story?**

Teachers' note Use the pictures to check the accuracy of the children's understanding. Discuss the characters and list words to describe them. What do the characters feel at different parts of the story? Investigate how stories are told from a point of view. What is the wolf's version? Is he really the villain? The choice of ending may reflect this. The children could think of alternative endings to other stories.

Developing Literacy
Text Level Year 4
© A & C Black 2000

Fiction and non-fiction

- **Read the two pieces of writing.**
- **Decide what they are about.**

Milk For The Cat

When the tea is brought at five o'clock,
And all the neat curtains are drawn with care,
The little black cat with bright green eyes
Is suddenly purring there.

HAROLD MONRO

Feeding a cat

It is normal for cats to be fussy with food to begin with. They usually like to eat:

- white meat
- chicken
- fish.

Cats drink water as well as milk.

- **Use the passages to complete the chart. It shows how fiction is different from non-fiction.**

	Fiction	**Non-fiction**
Purpose	To create a picture of a scene and a particular cat.	To give information about cats.
Subject		
Type of language (for example, descriptive, poetic, factual)		
Structure (for example, sentences, bullet points, rhymes, lists)		

Now try this!

- **Copy the first line of a story, a poem or a non-fiction text. Ask a partner to say which it is and to give reasons.**

Teachers' note Model with the children characteristics of the poem which are not in the factual passage and vice versa. Ask them to think of other examples of texts to back their views. They could look through books on a library shelf and sort them into fiction and non-fiction piles, giving their reasons.

Developing Literacy
Text Level Year 4
© A & C Black 2000

Fact or opinion?

- **Read what these children are saying. Label their views FACT or OPINION.**

I am nine years old.

_____

Our teacher is the best in the world.

_____

Smoking is a nasty habit.

_____

Mount Everest is the tallest mountain in the world.

_____

Mount Everest is the most beautiful mountain in the world.

_____

Smoking is an unhealthy habit.

_____

- **Read the extract from a non-fiction text about Ancient Egypt.**

- **Underline the facts in** red.

- **Underline the opinions in** blue.

Some sentences are a mixture of fact and opinion.

The pyramids of Egypt.

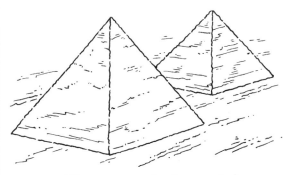

The most glorious sight in the world.

Cheops was a cruel king of the Fourth Dynasty. He built an ugly pyramid on the west bank of the Nile. It is 146.6m tall. Chephren, his much cleverer son, built his beautiful pyramid to the south of his father's. It is 3m lower. The third pyramid was built by Mycerinus. It is the smallest of the pyramids. It is much more mysterious. No mummies were found in the pyramids. I think they were stolen.

- **Use an information book to check that the facts are correct.**

Now try this!

- **Look in newspapers and magazines. Identify the facts and opinions in one article.**

Teachers' note Model with the children the first statement. How can they find out it is true? Is it an opinion or a fact? This should encourage the children to check their facts in reference books. Extend this work into point of view and reporting style. The children should become aware that eveything they see in print is not necessarily 'the truth'.

Developing Literacy
Text Level Year 4
© A & C Black 2000

A newspaper article

- **Read the newspaper article.**
- **Write the correct labels from the newspaper checklist in the boxes.**

Newspaper checklist

- Headline
- Sentence to introduce the story
- Paragraph to explain the story in more detail
- Simple description
- Subheading
- Direct speech
- Reported speech
- Photograph

PARTY BAN FOR TRAINING SHOES GIRL

Schoolgirl Tracy Smith was banned from her school disco because she was wearing training shoes.

Tracy, a Year 4 pupil at the local school, had taken her black shoes to be mended that day. 'All I had to wear was my trainers,' she said. She was not wearing proper school uniform so she was banned from the party.

While her classmates were enjoying themselves in the school hall, Tracy was left alone, crying in the playground.

Her mother, blonde 32 year-old scientist Maxine Smith from Jones Lane, Enfield, was very angry. 'This is the meanest trick ever played on a child,' she told us yesterday.

'My daughter was heartbroken. She came home and sobbed all night. She even left her chips on the plate.'

Unfair

Mrs Smith told us that she had gone to the school when her daughter phoned her. She tried to see the headteacher but she was dancing in the hall.

'I saw other children there wearing brown shoes, and the headteacher was wearing silver dancing shoes. It's not fair,' Mrs Smith shouted.

Now try this!

- **Write a brief newspaper article using the same features. Use this headline: SCHOOL CLOSED BY STRIKE**

Teachers' note This activity links with sentence-level work on the use of direct and reported speech. Model with the children what makes a newspaper article different from other texts in layout and language. Discuss the reasons for this. Children should realise that different kinds of newspaper articles may have different purposes, for example, some may argue a case, some may give facts.

**Developing Literacy
Text Level Year 4
© A & C Black 2000**

Headlines

- Write headlines to go with these pictures.

- Make notes about the kind of newspaper article which each of these headlines could introduce.

① **MANAGER SACKED AFTER MATCH**	Football story Team loses yet again
② **BEST TEACHER IN THE SCHOOL**	
③ **BAND SPLITS**	
④ *YEAR 4 GENIUS WINS PLACE*	

- Write up two of the stories using your notes.

Now try this!

- Some headlines can have more than one meaning. Re-write this headline twice to make its possible meanings clear.

BOY CHASES CAT WITH FISH

Teachers' note Look at headlines from a range of newspapers and ask children what stories they tell. How do they know? Investigate the idea that a good headline is a summary of the story. Model this, using well-known fables or nursery rhymes. As an additional extension activity, the children could re-write a nursery rhyme as a newspaper article.

Developing Literacy
Text Level Year 4
© A & C Black 2000

Instructions

- **Read the instructions. They are muddled up.**

IN CASE OF FIRE

Use the nearest safe exit.

Walk, do not run.

Make sure all doors and windows are closed.

Leave the building immediately.

Report to your teacher outside.

Call the fire brigade.

Line up in the playground.

Ensure no-one is left in the class.

Do not stop to collect your bag.

Ring the nearest fire alarm.

- **Re-write the instructions in the most sensible order. Number them.**
- **Why is it important to have instructions in the right order?**

IN CASE OF FIRE

1.

2.

- **Underline all the verbs in the instructions. What do you notice about them?** _____

Now try this!

- **Read some instructions for playing a game or for making something. Check that the instructions are in the right order and that the verbs are in the imperative (command form).**

Teachers' note This sheet serves to illustrate only two main points in instructional writing: chronological order and the use of imperative verbs. You may wish to investigate other kinds of instructional texts which use diagrams, technical vocabulary, an introduction to the reader, and perhaps a list of required items or ingredients.

Developing Literacy
Text Level Year 4
© A & C Black 2000

Arguments

When you write an argument you are giving your point of view.

- **Read this passage.**
- **Is the author for or against the subject?**
- **In the chart, write the arguments the author uses.**
- **Underline the words the writer uses to join the arguments (for example, 'however').**

> I think children should not be allowed to wear ear-rings in school. They are dangerous. If you wear one in PE you might get it torn out and be hurt. Wearing ear-rings also proves you are showing off in school. However, some parents buy their children jewellery, so they have to wear it. For example, my friend Wayne has four gold ear-rings. To conclude, wearing ear-rings should not be allowed. It makes less well-off children jealous and causes trouble. Therefore, it should be written in the school rules.

Arguments for	Arguments against

- **Write arguments opposing the author's point of view in the chart.**

Teachers' note Model with the children the features of an argument in a shared text. Make a point that this is one form of writing which often uses the present tense. The children could write an argument as a speech to persuade the class about a point of view.

Developing Literacy
Text Level Year 4
© A & C Black 2000

Discussions

When you write a discussion, you need to present all sides of an argument, not just what you think.

- **Read the passage.**
- **Circle the words the writer uses to join the points of view.**

Some adults think that children are not old enough to come to school on their own. They say that it is dangerous to cross the road. Other people agree with them and point to the number of children hurt on the roads. But children disagree. They show they can be responsible every day in school. They learn to cross roads when they are very young. Also, they argue, parents in cars block the roads near the schools, which is dangerous. My opinion is that most children can come to school on their own. They just have to be taught about the dangers.

- **Write the arguments for and against allowing children to come to school on their own.**

For	Against

Now try this!

- **Underline the verbs in the discussion text. Which is the main tense?** _____
- **Write your own views on the subject.**

Teachers' note Writing a discussion text should be a natural extension of debate. Model with the children the features of a discussion in a shared text and bring out the difference between a discussion and an argument (see page 47). Make a point that this is one form of writing which often uses the present tense.

Developing Literacy
Text Level Year 4
© A & C Black 2000

Explanation ladder

- **Use the ladder to help you plan an explanation.**

The purpose of my explanation:

Explanations are usually written in the present tense.

Think about the kinds of words you will use to join the steps together (for example, 'next' or 'then').

Introduction

Step 1

Step 2

Step 3

Conclusion

Now try this!

- **Write the explanation in paragraphs, using the notes from your ladder.**
- **Explanations often have diagrams. What diagrams would be helpful to your reader?**

Teachers' note Explanations need to be clear, structured and focused to achieve their purpose; this sheet should enable children to scaffold their writing on any instructional text. Discuss how best to use connectives to join the paragraphs in a logical and stylish way. Test out instructions; ask the children to follow them precisely and suggest improvements.

Developing Literacy
Text Level Year 4
© A & C Black 2000

Advertisements

- **Read the advertisement.**
- **Write the correct labels from the advertisement checklist in the boxes.**

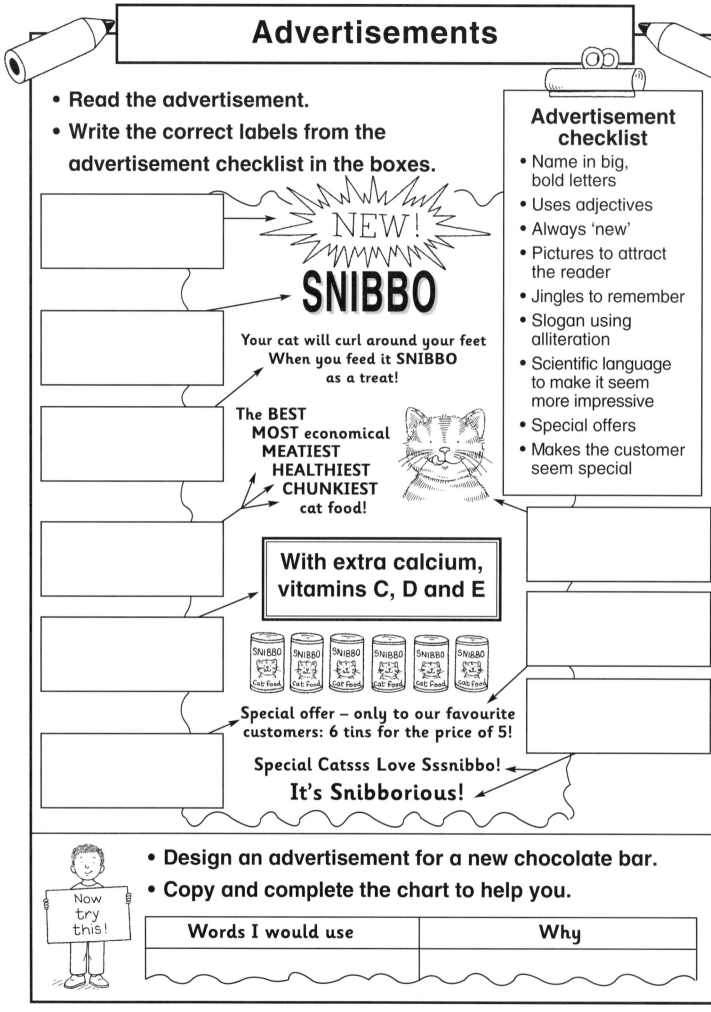

Advertisement checklist
- Name in big, bold letters
- Uses adjectives
- Always 'new'
- Pictures to attract the reader
- Jingles to remember
- Slogan using alliteration
- Scientific language to make it seem more impressive
- Special offers
- Makes the customer seem special

NEW!

SNIBBO

Your cat will curl around your feet
When you feed it SNIBBO
as a treat!

The BEST
  MOST economical
  MEATIEST
   HEALTHIEST
    CHUNKIEST
    cat food!

With extra calcium, vitamins C, D and E

Special offer – only to our favourite customers: 6 tins for the price of 5!

Special Catsss Love Sssnibbo!
It's Snibborious!

Now try this!

- **Design an advertisement for a new chocolate bar.**
- **Copy and complete the chart to help you.**

Words I would use	Why

Teachers' note Model with the children what makes an advertisement different from other texts in its layout. Discuss the reasons for these features. It is important for children to realise that an advertisement is aiming to persuade them. This links with sentence-level work on the use of adjectives. The children could look for the same features in other magazine advertisements.

Developing Literacy
Text Level Year 4
© A & C Black 2000

Language to persuade

- **Read this page from a holiday brochure. Underline the words which try to persuade you.**
- **Read the questions surrounding the text.**
- **What information does the brochure NOT give you? Why do you think this might be?**

Is it miles away from the village?

How many rooms are there?

The holiday of your dreams

This fabulous, luxury, friendly, family hotel has its own beachfront at the quieter end of the bay. It is only a tiny walk from the golden sands and a short hop from the colourful, unspoilt village. The wonderful views are what make this hotel such a glorious, relaxing place in which to stay.

  Some rooms have spacious balconies, and most of these enjoy stunning sea views. All the rooms are simply but tastefully furnished.

  Freda and Max, the owners, create a warm, friendly environment in which guests can relax in comfort.

Does it have a pool?

How many rooms have a sea view?

Does the hotel have a restaurant?

- **Underline in** red **all the adjectives used.**
  Write them in a chart like this one.

Adjectives which give a good feeling	Adjectives which give a bad feeling

- **Underline in** blue **all the facts you are given.**
  How many are there? _____

Now try this!

- **Change some of the positive adjectives to their opposites. What happens?**
- **Re-write the description to show the hotel as an unpleasant place.**

Teachers' note It is important that children are aware that information can be used to persuade them to buy something. Information can have purposes other than merely to inform. Children could write excerpts from their own holiday brochures, perhaps about the school. They could write postcards home from the hotel above, describing what it is really like.

Developing Literacy
Text Level Year 4
© A & C Black 2000

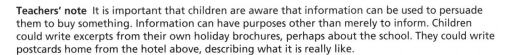

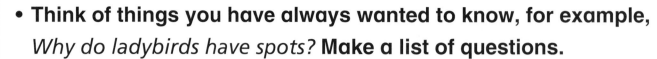

Preparing for research

- **Think of things you have always wanted to know, for example,** *Why do ladybirds have spots?* **Make a list of questions.**
- **Use this sheet to prepare for your research into each question.**

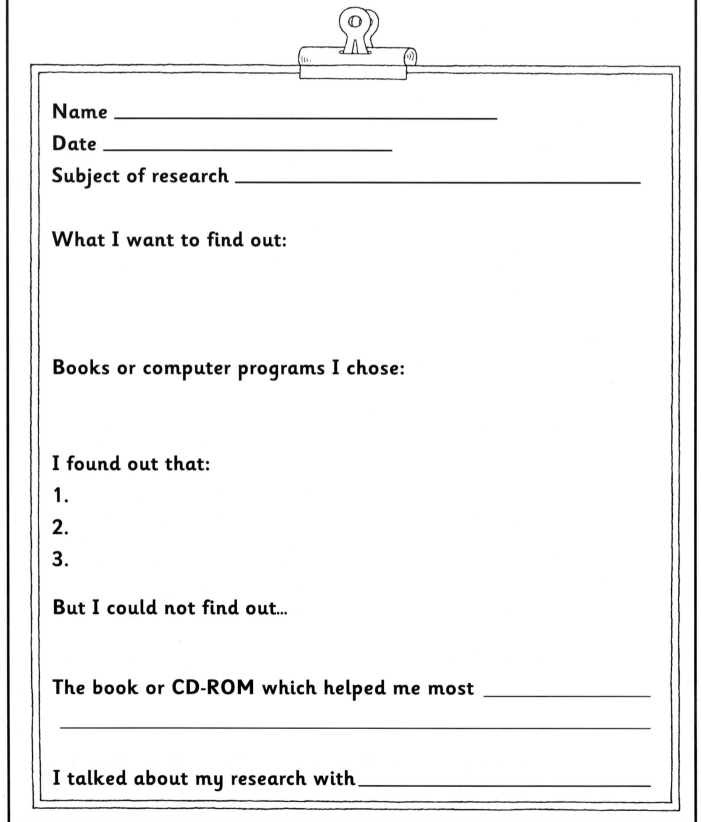

Name _____

Date _____

Subject of research _____

What I want to find out:

Books or computer programs I chose:

I found out that:

1.

2.

3.

But I could not find out...

The book or CD-ROM which helped me most _____

_____

I talked about my research with _____

Teachers' note This sheet could be used to structure research into any curriculum area. Children need to communicate what they do not know as well as what they do. In this way they can find the best sources of information to answer their questions. You could create a wall display of the sheets, each week focusing on areas of research so that the children can help one another.

Developing Literacy
Text Level Year 4
© A & C Black 2000

Key words

To make notes, you need to pick out the most important points.
These are called key words .

- **Read the passage.**
- **Write the rest of the key words in the diagram.**

The dog is the best-known and best-loved animal in the world. Scientists believe that dogs are related to the wolf family. There are many different breeds of dog – all shapes and sizes. Dogs are very intelligent animals. Many, for example police dogs, work with humans. The dog is a faithful companion.

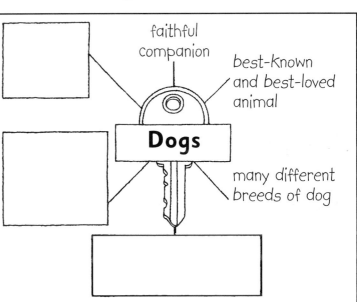

faithful companion

best-known and best-loved animal

Dogs

many different breeds of dog

- **Read this passage. Write the key words in the diagram.**

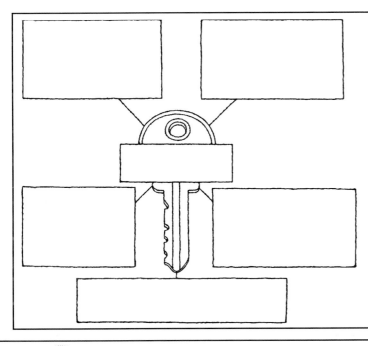

The first postage stamps were issued in Britain in 1840. Poor people could not afford them. Postage was charged according to weight and the distance a letter had to travel. The first stamps cost one old penny (the Penny Black) and two old pennies (the Twopenny Blue), paid in advance. In 1842, stamps were introduced in America.

Now try this!

- **Use a passage from a non-fiction book. Make your own key words diagram and add the words.**

Teachers' note This is a diagrammatic method of note-taking. You could ask the children to take the same passages and underline key points to see if they result in the same facts being extracted. The important aspect of note-taking is to make children aware that they should write what they have discovered in their own words – not simply copy out what the book tells them.

Developing Literacy
Text Level Year 4
© A & C Black 2000

Charts and diagrams

- **Read the information about Hindu gods and goddesses.**

Name	God or goddess of...	Special features
Brahma	Creation	Four heads facing different ways, holds spoon, book, beads, water
Laksmi	Prosperity	Hands in giving position, holds lotus flowers, drops money
Sarasvati	Wisdom, learning	Rises from a lotus flower, plays musical instrument
Shiva	Creation and destruction	Three lines on forehead, carries a trident
Vishnu	Preserver of the world	Carries discus and mace, holds conch shell and lotus

- **Match the pictures to the correct gods and goddesses.**
- **Name them. Then write two clues which helped you.**

1 Laksmi 2 3 4 5

Clues		Sarasvati	1 _____
Brahma 1 _____			2 _____
2 _____		**Shiva**	1 _____
Laksmi 1 _____			2 _____
2 _____		**Vishnu**	1 _____
			2 _____

Now try this!

- **Find out about gods and goddesses of ancient Greece.**
- **Make a chart like the one above. Draw labelled pictures of the gods and goddesses from the information.**

Teachers' note This is an opportunity to link with other areas of the curriculum, such as RE and history. Try reversing the process on this sheet. Give the children pictures and ask them to make a table from the information they can find.

Developing Literacy
Text Level Year 4
© A & C Black 2000

Writing a newspaper article

- **Use this planner to help you to write a newspaper article.**

Write your headline here.

Write your introductory sentence. Say what the story will be about. Mention people's names.

Write a longer paragraph to explain your introductory sentence.

What details of simple description will you use?

Write some subheadings to tell your reader what the parts of the story are about.

Write some direct speech – some quotations from the people involved.

Write some of these speeches in reported speech.

- **Use your notes to write the article.**
- **Ask a partner to say if your article sounds like a real newspaper article. Make changes.**

Teachers' note Model with the children the characteristics of a newspaper article, either in a shared text or from page 44. The children could use this sheet as a format to make notes and to discuss the characteristics of real articles. It is important that the children draft their work, taking note of comment. They could produce a newspaper of all the articles, printed from a word-processing file.

Developing Literacy
Text Level Year 4
© A & C Black 2000

Writing instructions

Instructions tell someone how to do or make something.

- **Use this sheet to help you to write instructions.**

Word-bank
First
Then
After that
Next
Finally

This is how to

You will need

Stage 1

Stage 2

Stage 3

Stage 4

Now try this!

- **Write a set of instructions using your notes. Add any diagrams which you think would be helpful.**
- **Underline the verbs. What do you notice?**

Teachers' note In pairs, ask the children to carry out each other's instructions precisely in order to show if any stages are missing. This can be made into a fun game. In this way they will come to realise the importance of correct sequencing and also of having the correct materials or information to carry out the instructions.

Developing Literacy
Text Level Year 4
© A & C Black 2000

Writing a report

Reports describe the way things are.

- **Use this planner to help you write a report on keeping a pet.**

What pet will you keep?

Reports need detail to make them clear.

1. Write three facts about your pet.

2. What will you feed it? How often?

Draw a picture of your pet here.

5. Any other information, for example, how will you clean your pet's home?

3. How will you house it? What are the reasons for this?

4. How many will you have? What are the reasons for this?

Now try this!

- **Write your report using your notes. Add any diagrams which you think would be helpful.**
- **What tense will you use to write your report?**

Teachers' note This sheet could be used as a stimulus for research, that is, *what information do I need to find?* Or it could be used to scaffold writing after research has been completed. Discuss the characteristics of reports: use of the present tense, diagrams to help, talking generally about the subject (pronouns such as 'they') but using detail to illustrate the idea.

Developing Literacy
Text Level Year 4
© A & C Black 2000

Writing an explanation

This strange machine is making the holes in middle of CDs!

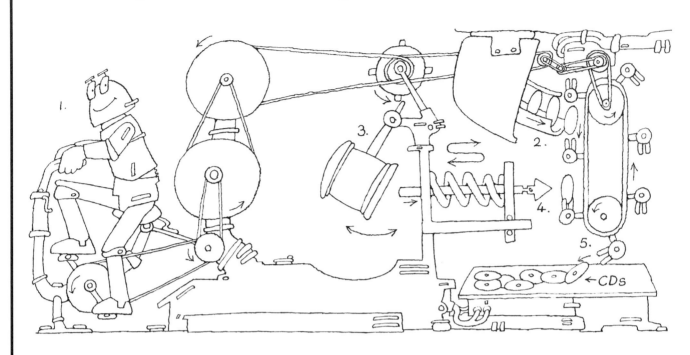

- **Explain how the machine works. Think of the order in which different parts work.**

1. <u>A robot pushes pedals to turn the wheels which keep the machine moving.</u>

2. _____
_____

3. _____
_____

4. _____
_____

5. _____
_____

Now try this!

- **Design your own strange-looking machine for doing something useful.**
- **Explain how it works.**

Teachers' note Discuss the picture with the children and start the process by questioning them and writing their responses on the board. Bring them to an awareness that when you are explaining a process, the details need to be in chronological order otherwise the process will not make sense to the reader.

Developing Literacy
Text Level Year 4
© A & C Black 2000

Writing an advertisement

Use this planner to help you to write an advertisement.

- Invent a name for your product. Use big, bold letters.

NEW!

Make a list of adjectives to describe your product.

What pictures will you use?

What scientific words can you find to help your product sound better?

Write a slogan using alliteration.

Write a rhyme to help people remember your product.

What words will make your customer feel like someone special?

Now try this!

- Design your advertisement and show it to a friend.
- Does it make your friend want to buy your product?
- Make changes.

Teachers' note The class could create an entire advertising campaign and organise the roles necessary for this, such as designer and copy-writer. The children could research television advertising, using this page to help collect data. Discuss what works for children, that is, what makes them want to buy something and what does not. You could create a class display of their campaign.

Developing Literacy
Text Level Year 4
© A & C Black 2000

Making notes

Seat belts save lives.

- **Read this Government leaflet telling us to wear seat belts.**

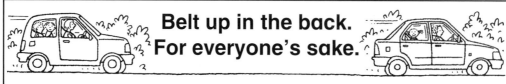

Belt up in the back. For everyone's sake.

The law says:

You must wear a seat belt in a car. A driver can be taken to court if a child under 14 does not wear one.

Any child in the front seat of a car must wear a belt or some kind of restraint.

If children under three are in the front seat of a car, they must be put in a proper child restraint. In the back seat, they must wear a restraint if there is one, or a seat belt.

If there is a restraint or belt in the front (and not in the back), children between 3 and 11 (and under 1.5m tall) must be put in it.

ADAPTED FROM THE LEAFLET 'SEAT BELTS AND CHILD RESTRAINTS' ISSUED BY THE DETR

- **Write the information from the leaflet on the chart.**

	In the front seat?	In the back seat?	Who is responsible?
Driver	Must wear seat belt	—	
Children under 3	Child restraint		
Children 3–11 (under 1.5m tall)			
Children 12 or 13 (over 1.5m tall)			
Grown-up passengers	Must wear seat belt	Must wear seat belt	Passenger

Now try this!

- **Write a paragraph to explain the use of seat belts. Use only the notes you made on the chart.**

Teachers' note The children should realise that there are various ways of extracting relevant information. Compare with page 53. It is important that they re-cast their information in their own words and do not simply copy out passages from the text. Ask children to compare what information they have taken from the original.

Developing Literacy
Text Level Year 4
© A & C Black 2000

From notes to a paragraph

- **Read these notes, which were made by a police officer.**

Mr Barker – woken up –
6.30am – noises – dining room.
Got up – opened door – saw
two men – carrying video – one
saw him – dropped video – ran
into garden – over wall – into
next garden. Mr Barker chased
him – thief lost trainer – man
too fast – Mr Barker went
home – phoned police –
checked for missing things –
police arrived 7.30am.

- **Write the notes as a report.**

POLICE REPORT

Name of officer: _____   Date: _____

Events:

_____

_____

_____

_____

_____

_____

_____

_____

_____

_____

Now try this!

- **Write notes from a notice which lists your school rules.**
- **Write a report on the rules for a new pupil coming to the school.**

Teachers' note Discuss abbreviations used in note-taking and what these mean. This can link with word derivation at word level. Make a list of these abbreviations and display them in the class for constant use. Concentrate on how the children can link the notes to make a flowing and coherent narrative for a reader who does not know the background.

Developing Literacy
Text Level Year 4
© A & C Black 2000

Summarising

- **Read this passage about being a guest in a Japanese home.**
- **Write notes to summarise the most important facts.**

You could underline the facts first to decide which are the most important.

If you are invited to a meal in a Japanese home you must take off your shoes when you go inside.

Meals will consist of many small dishes. You may think they are strange – especially those with raw fish.

Be polite. You should try some of the food. Your Japanese friends will not be upset if you leave the food.

A meal will finish with fruit. When your Japanese friends think it is time for you to go, they may say that your car is waiting. This is not being rude.

After a day or two, you should write a letter of thanks to your Japanese hosts.

The most important facts

Paragraph 1

Paragraph 2

Paragraph 3

Paragraph 4

Paragraph 5

Now try this!

- **Write three paragraphs for a foreign visitor explaining how to be a polite guest in your house.**
- **Ask a friend to summarise the points you make.**

Teachers' note Selecting the most important facts is a difficult procedure. Try inventing games in which you introduce silly statements into a serious text so that the children can see what is obviously irrelevant. Paired work also gives the children an opportunity to take feedback and edit their work.

Developing Literacy
Text Level Year 4
© A & C Black 2000